I0808279

"Comfort, comfort my people,"
says your God,
"Speak comfort to Jerusalem, and cry out to her,
That her warfare is ended,
That her sin is pardoned."

Isaiah 40:1-2

[Hear] the voice of one crying in the wilderness:
"Prepare the way of the LORD;
Make straight in the desert
A highway for our God.
Every valley shall be exalted
And every mountain and hill brought low;
The crooked places shall be made straight
And the rough places smooth.
The glory of the LORD shall be revealed,
And all flesh shall see it together;
For the mouth of the LORD has spoken."

Isaiah 40:3-5

Behold, the virgin shall be with child,
and bear a son, And they shall call
his name Immanuel,
which is translated, "God with us."

Matthew 1:23

For unto us a child is born,
Unto us a son is given;
And the government will be upon his shoulder.
And his name will be called
Wonderful, Counselor, Mighty God,
Everlasting Father, Prince of Peace.

Isaiah 9:6

There were shepherds keeping watch over
their flock by night. And behold, an angel of the
Lord stood before them, and the glory of the Lord
shone around them, and they were greatly afraid.

Luke 2:8-9

Then the angel said to them, "Do not be afraid, for behold, I bring you good tidings of great joy which will be to all people. For there is born to you this day in the city of David a Savior, who is Christ the Lord."

Luke 2:10-11

And this will be the sign to you: You will find a babe wrapped in swaddling cloths, lying in a manger. And suddenly there was with the angel a multitude of the heavenly host praising God and saying: "Glory to God in the highest, And on earth peace, goodwill toward men!"

Luke 2:12-14

He will feed his flock like a shepherd;
He will gather the lambs with his arm,
And carry them in his bosom,
And gently lead those who are with young.

Isaiah 40:11

[But] all we like sheep have gone astray;
We have turned, every one, to his own way;
And the LORD has laid on him the sin of us all.

Isaiah 53:6

He was despised and rejected by men,
A man of sorrows and acquainted with grief.
Surely he has borne our griefs
And carried our sorrows;
But he was wounded for our transgressions,
He was bruised for our sins;
The chastisement for our peace was upon him,
And by his stripes we are healed.

Isaiah 53:3-5

Reproach has broken my heart,
And I am full of heaviness;
I looked for someone to take pity, but there was none;
And for comforters, but I found none.

Psalm 69:20

Behold and see if there is any sorrow
like unto my sorrow.

Lamentations 1:12

Behold the Lamb of God,
Who takes away the sin of the world.

John 1:29

Then shall be brought to pass the saying that is written:
"Death is swallowed up in victory.
O Death, where is your sting?
O Grave, where is your victory?"
But thanks be to God, who gives us the victory through
our Lord Jesus Christ.

1 Corinthians 15:54-55, 57

For I know that my Redeemer lives,
And He shall stand at last on the earth;
And after my skin is destroyed, this I know,
That in my flesh I shall see God.

Job 19:25-26

But now Christ is risen from the dead.
For since by man came death,
by man also came the resurrection of the dead.
For as in Adam all die, even so in Christ all
shall be made alive.

1 Corinthians 15:20-22

How beautiful are the feet of those
who preach the gospel of peace,
Who bring glad tidings of good things.

Romans 10:15

Their sound has gone out to all the earth,
And their words to the ends of the world.

Romans 10:18

The kingdoms of this world have become the kingdoms of our Lord and of His Christ, and He shall reign forever and ever!

Revelation 11:15

Hallelujah! For the Lord God
Omnipotent reigns!

Revelation 19:6